NATIVE AMERICAN CULTURE

BY KATHERINE GLEASON

Rourke
Publishing LLC
Vero Beach, Florida 32964

Developed by Nancy Hall, Inc., for Rourke Publishing.
© 2006 Nancy Hall, Inc.

Acknowledgments are listed on page 48.

www.rourkepublishing.com

Photo research by L. C. Casterline
Design by Atif Toor and Iram Khandwala

Library of Congress Cataloging-In-Publication Data

Gleason, Katherine.
  Native American culture / by Katherine Gleason.
      p. cm. -- (Discovering the arts)
  Includes bibliographical references and index.
  ISBN 1-59515-522-8 (hardcover)
  1. Indian arts--North America. 2. Indian architecture--North America. 3.
Indian painting--North America. 4. Indian music--North America. 5. Indian
sculpture--North America. 6. Indian literature--North America. I. Title.
II. Series.
  E98.A73G54 2006
  704.03'97--dc22

                              2005010733

Title page: Masked Dancers, Kwakiutl Culture.
During a *t'seka*, or winter dance, which was performed at feasts called potlatches,
the Kwakiutl wore masks to act out legends.

Printed in the USA
10 9 8 7 6 5 4 3 2 1

CONTENTS

A WAY OF LIFE

Creating beautiful things has been an important part of Native American culture for thousands of years. Traditionally, Native American art was not made to hang on a wall in a museum. Instead, simple objects that were made for everyday use were crafted with such care, they became works of art in themselves.

Art objects, such as masks, were created for religious ceremonies. Other kinds of objects were created with the same care and respect. For example, when crafting a **kayak** the Arctic people sing and pray to make sure the boat is well made.

The Bella Coola sun mask may be worn by a dancer or set up to move across the back wall of the dancing hall to represent the rising and setting of the sun.

Native Americans have also created art to trade or sell among different **tribes**, as well as to visitors. In some cases, new types of art were created especially to sell to tourists.

Today, Native American artists help to preserve the traditions of many tribes. They are also breaking new ground and creating new traditions. Native American art is a living art that will continue to grow and thrive.

The Plains people moved often, following the buffalo herds. Tipis, which were made of buffalo hide and supported by poles, could be easily taken down, carried, and put back up in another place.

An Inuit man paddles a kayak in this photograph from the early 1900s.

CHAPTER 1

THE EASTERN TRIBES

In early times, many Native Americans who lived east of the Mississippi River buried their dead in earthen mounds. Along with the dead, they buried beads, carved pipes, and other artworks. In fact, most of the artwork that survives has been found in burial mounds.

Some of the oldest pieces date back to 3000 B.C.E. Among them are carved stone weights that were attached to spear-throwers called atlatls. Some of the atlatl weights are very beautiful. The craftsmen who made these weights probably meant them to be displayed, traded, or used as funeral offerings.

Tobacco was the first crop planted by Native North Americans. They have used it in religious rites since

This carved stone pipe was found in an Adena burial mound in Ohio. It may have belonged to a **shaman**, or holy man.

1500 B.C.E. In many cultures, tobacco was smoked in stone pipes that were carved in the shape of animals and people.

Early Native Americans also made beads, carvings, and sculptures from wood, seashells, and copper. The Copper Culture people lived around Lake Superior. They were among the first people in the world to make forged copper tools. They also made copper jewelry, such as bracelets and rings.

To make this image of a falcon from the Ohio Hopewell culture, copper nuggets were beaten into flat sheets, heated, and cut into shape.

The Serpent Mound in southern Ohio is 1,330 feet (405 m) long. **Archaeologists**, people who study ancient cultures, first thought that the Adena people built it. Now some of them believe it was built by the Fort Ancient people, who lived there from C.E. 1000 to 1550.

This beautiful wood bowl in the shape of a beaver was traded in northwestern Ohio, where many tribes mixed, including the Kaskaskia, Shawnee, and Miami. It dates back to the late 1700s.

By the 1580s, French traders had begun visiting the East Coast of North America. Huron hunters exchanged beaver pelts for glass beads, iron nails, and metal blades to make axes and knives. They also used these improved tools to carve wooden bowls, spoons, masks, and other objects. In the late 1700s, men from many tribes, including the Iroquois, Shawnee, Miami, and Ojibwa, carved wooden feast bowls. Some of these bowls were shaped like beavers to honor the animals whose fur had brought them wealth.

Sequoyah, a silversmith, created a writing system for the Cherokee language. He used 86 symbols to stand for the different sounds. In 1821, the system was approved by the Cherokee tribal council. *The Cherokee Phoenix* became the first Native American newspaper published in the United States in 1828. It was printed in both Cherokee and English.

Sequoyah's Cherokee alphabet was called "Talking Leaves."

The Trail of Tears
by Robert Lindneux

As more Europeans came to America, they began to fight with the tribes for control over land. In 1830, the Indian Removal Act was passed. Under this law, many Native Americans were ordered to leave their homes and move west to make room for the new settlers. The Cherokee people were forced to walk from Georgia to Oklahoma. This forced march came to be known as the Trail of Tears, because about 4,000 Cherokee died along the way.

Pictured on this Mesquakie bag are two Underwater Panthers, beings that were believed to whip up storms with their long tails.

The women of the tribes made clothes, baskets, and pots. Often, they decorated clothing with beads. In early times, they made their own beads using bone, shells, stones, horn, teeth, ivory, clay, gold, silver, copper, pearls, seeds, wood, and porcupine quills. After Europeans arrived, glass beads became popular. They were easy to get, so the women began to use more beads in their work. Some clothing created in the late 1800s was almost completely covered with beads. These clothes, hats, moccasins, and other items were worn on special occasions.

Beads were sewn in lots of different patterns. Ottawa women created designs such as the Thunderbird and the Underwater Panther, which are important spiritual beings. By the early 1900s, Ojibwa women designed beaded flower patterns. They were based on the floral embroidery the women had learned from European nuns at school.

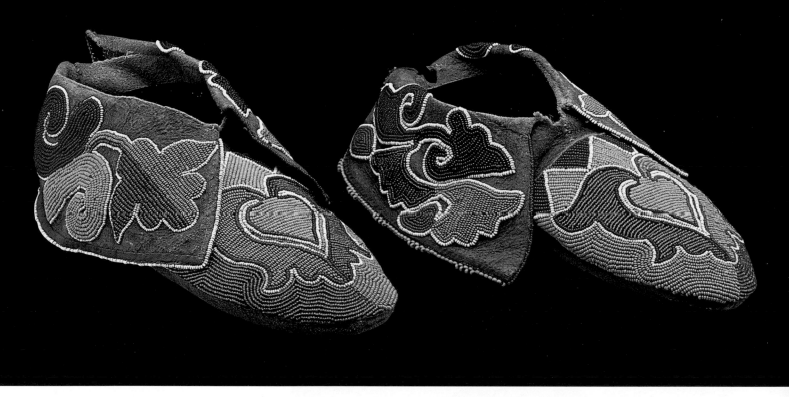

These Iowa moccasins were made in about 1860. They are embroidered with colorful glass beads in the prairie style.

After the Eastern tribes were forced to move west to **reservations**, they came in contact with the Cheyenne, Kiowa, and other Plains tribes. The women learned from each other and came up with new bead designs known as the "prairie style." Bright colors in flower patterns became popular among the Iowa, Cherokee, Delaware, and Osage tribes. Some women started making beadwork, clothing, and dolls to sell to whites.

CHAPTER 2

THE PLAINS TRIBES

Early life on the plains was hard. The tribes moved around, following the herds of buffalo that the men hunted. Some tribes, such as the Blackfoot, used dogs pulling travois (a type of sled) to carry their things. Later, they used horses. Because the people moved so frequently, there was not much time to make art. But there was always time for storytelling.

By 1700, life on the plains began to change forever. The cause of this great change came from Europe. It was the horse.

A long, long time ago, the Creator shaped handfuls of mud into humans. Then he blew on them, and they came alive. The Creator taught people how to hunt and collect wild foods, but still, the people were often hungry. They found a place where there were lots of animals to hunt. Unfortunately, there were also enormous animals that ate people. To be safe, the people hid in caves. More and more people were born. After many years, there were so many people that the giant animals were afraid. Then the people came out of their caves and lived in the open.

For centuries, the Cheyenne people have told this creation story. It was not until the mid-1900s, however, that the story was written down by a Cheyenne man named John Stands In Timber. He wanted to make sure that it would always be remembered.

In addition to telling stories, the early Plains people also made things that they could carry easily, such as pipes, small sculptures (above), and pots.

This Sioux shirt from South Dakota was made in the 1870s. It is decorated with glass beads, horse hair, human hair, and porcupine quills.

Once the Plains people got horses, hunting was easier, and there was more time to make art. Traditionally, women made clothes from animal hides. First, they scraped off the flesh, fat, and hair. Then they softened the hides and sewed them to make moccasins, shirts, and leggings. In early times, they used dyed porcupine quills to decorate their clothing. Later, they used small numbers of large glass beads, which they got through trade with whites. By the mid-1800s, small glass beads in lots of different colors were plentiful.

Besides clothing, women used beadwork to decorate cases for knives and spears. And, of course, they made beadwork to decorate the horses. The designs women created with beads were usually based on

Some Cheyenne headdresses were so long that a warrior could only wear one while mounted on his horse.

geometric figures, like rectangles and triangles. By the late 1800s, however, women began to make designs that showed pictures of men on horseback.

Beadwork was also used to decorate the brow bands of warbonnets. These were usually made with eagle feathers and worn by warriors from many Plains tribes, including the Cheyenne, Comanche, Nez Percé, and Sioux. A warrior had to earn the right to wear a feather bonnet through acts of bravery.

Hin-mah-too-yah-lat-kekt of the Nez Percé became known as Chief Joseph. After gold was found and white settlers began moving in, the government took back nine-tenths of the reservation in Idaho and Oregon. When the Nez Percé refused to move, fighting broke out. In October 1877, the badly outnumbered tribe surrendered. In a speech that would become famous, Chief Joseph said, "I am tired of fighting . . . My heart is sick and sad. From where the sun now stands I will fight no more forever."

Traditionally, Plains men used paint to decorate their clothing, shields, and horses. They made paint from ground minerals, clay, and plants. They painted spiritual and mythic beings, such as Zemoguani, the Kiowa horned fish. The men also used symbols to represent their status in battle. Pipes stood for the number of war parties they had been in. Hands represented blows struck against an enemy. Sometimes a man used a splotch of red paint to show where he had been wounded.

As Plains tribes came into closer contact with white artists such as George Catlin and Karl Bodmer, their drawings changed. The men started making drawings of themselves in battle. At first, they painted on hides. Then, they started using ledger books like the ones the settlers used for bookkeeping. Ledger book art become a way for the Plains people to record their traditions and history.

As more and more wagon trains of settlers crossed the

The pictures on this buffalo robe from the upper Missouri River area show its original owner taking part in many different battles.

plains, the territory of the buffalo was divided in two. Fights over territory between tribes and with the United States government were common. Because of overhunting by white settlers, almost all of the buffalo were gone by 1880. The old Plains way of life came to an end, but not all the traditions were lost. Some were kept alive in Wild West shows. Plains men dressed in heavily beaded costumes and showed off their great abilities with horses.

The Crow Chief Arapoosh lived from about 1790 to 1834, when he was killed in battle. A figure representing the moon appears on his war shield. Among the objects attached are a crane's head, feathers, buffalo hide, and deerskin.

Many Kiowa, Cheyenne, Comanche, and Arapaho warriors refused to move to the lands that the government had set aside for Native American tribes. Reservations were usually areas that white settlers did not think were good enough and did not want. In 1874, the warriors were sent to prison in Florida. The prisoners produced hundreds of drawings, which were sold to tourists. The drawing of two warriors at left was made by Etahdleuh Doanmoe, a young Kiowa warrior.

CHAPTER 3

THE SOUTHWESTERN TRIBES

Native people have lived in the Southwest since at least 6000 B.C.E. Even though it is very dry there, people had begun farming by 300 B.C.E. The Anasazi created terraced fields that saved water and helped them grow food. Today, they are famous for their architecture. Some of the large, many-storied adobe houses that they built still stand today.

The Spanish who traveled to the area in 1540 called the farming villages pueblos. Today, people continue to live in pueblos in New Mexico and Arizona. These pueblos are the oldest places still used as homes in North America.

Deep in Canyon del Muerto in Arizona are the ruins of an Anasazi pueblo, which was deserted around 1270. Named Antelope House, after some nearby paintings on a cliff wall, the pueblo may once have had as many as 91 rooms.

This human-shaped piece was made by an Anasazi potter between the 900s and 1200s. The word *Anasazi* is Navajo for "the ancestors of our enemies."

For the people of the Southwest, art has always been a key part of religious practice. The Navajo hold the Night **Chant** to bring a sick person back into balance. During the eight-and-a-half-day ceremony, a shaman creates a sand painting. The person who is sick sits in the middle of the finished painting. The sand is rubbed on the sick person's body to help him or her soak up the healing powers of the spirit world. The last prayer of the Night Chant ends like this:

May it be beautiful before me.
May it be beautiful behind me.
May it be beautiful below me.
May it be beautiful all around me.
In beauty it is finished.
In beauty it is finished.

The people of the Southwest began to make pottery in about C.E. 400. They made clay pots to hold water and food. They also made pots for religious uses, such as funeral offerings, and to trade for other goods.

Young women learned to make pots from their relatives. First they dug up the clay. Then they prepared and kneaded it until it was smooth. They formed long snakes from the clay and coiled these to form pots. Then they smoothed the sides. Pots were hardened by placing them in the center of an outdoor fire. The painting and decoration of a pot was up to the individual. Older women encouraged younger women to find designs for their pots in their dreams.

Nampeyo was a famous potter from the Tewa-Hopi tribe. Her designs were inspired by ancient pots. She looked for **shards**, or broken pieces, of old pots near her home and studied them. Nampeyo was one of the

The Salado culture was a mix of peoples, including Mogollon, Hohokam, and Anasazi. This pottery canteen made between 1300 and 1350 is shaped like a duck but has a human face.

first Native Americans to be recognized as an artist by whites. In 1910, she was called "the greatest maker of Indian pottery alive." Today, Nampeyo's pots are priced as high as $20,000.

Tourists visited the Hopi village of Hano on First Mesa in Arizona to watch the potter Nampeyo work and to buy her pots.

In the early 1900s, Maria Martinez of San Ildefonso Pueblo in New Mexico built pots and her husband, Julian, painted them. The couple became well known all over the world for their pottery. They worked together until Julian's death in 1943 and won many awards for their inventive black-on-black designs. Maria continued making pots until she died in 1980.

The early Pueblo people wove cotton threads on upright looms to make cloth for beautifully decorated shawls. In 1598, Spanish settlers began moving to the area, bringing sheep with them. Soon the Pueblo began to weave with wool.

The Navajo learned to weave from the Pueblo. At first, they made shawls in the same style as the Pueblo. Then they developed their own styles. By 1800, the Navajo were making striped blankets called "chiefs' blankets," because only chiefs could afford them. These blankets were worn over the shoulders. They were very popular, especially among the Plains tribes. Selling these blankets became an important way for the Navajo to make money.

Created between 1885 and 1895, this brightly colored Navajo blanket was woven with geometric designs in the "eye dazzler" style.

Taken in 1892 or 1893, this photograph shows a Navajo woman weaving a blanket at a camp in Kean's Canyon, Arizona. The woman at left is spinning wool, the woman at right is weaving a belt, and the child is carding wool.

In 1864, about 8,000 Navajo were forced to walk 300 miles (483 km) to the Bosque Redondo reservation on the Pecos River. The water was bad and food was scarce. Many people got sick or starved. Despite the hardship, Navajo artists created blankets in bright new zigzag patterns to sell to whites. They wove these designs with yarn that was given to them by the government. By 1868, life on the reservation was so bad that the Navajo were allowed to return home. When trains started coming to the Southwest in 1880, tourists began to buy Navajo blankets. Navajo weavers became known all over the world as great artists.

Although **kachina tihus** look like dolls, they are not. They are tools that Hopi and Zuni children use to learn about their religion. A kachina tihu is a carving that represents a **kachina**, the spirit of a living thing. Kwahu is the eagle kachina, and Avachhoya is the corn kachina. There are more than 300 kinds of kachinas.

Kachina tihus are usually carved from dried roots of the cottonwood tree. After the carver finds a good root, he uses a chisel and a knife to shape the wood. Then he sands it smooth. He paints the root and finally attaches cloth, feathers, and fur.

Kachinas are also represented by men dressed in costumes during sacred dances. Kachina dances are held every year between the months of December and July. After 1920, some native artists began to make kachina tihus to sell to tourists. Some Hopi and Zuni people think that selling kachina tihus has weakened the tribes' connection with the spirits.

Though Zuni law did not allow kachina tihus to be sold, early 20th-century carvers secretly created and sold 73 of them to the Brooklyn Museum.

Atsidi Sani was the first Navajo to create silver jewelry. He learned to work with silver in 1853. In the early days of jewelry making, Navajo craftsmen melted down silver coins. Then they formed the metal into jewelry. After traders started to sell their work to tourists, jewelry makers used sheets of silver and precut turquoise stones.

A 19th-century Navajo silversmith (above) holds a belt of conchas, silver disks threaded together with leather. His tools can be seen at right.

Navajo necklaces, like this one from the early 1900s, are called "squash-blossom" necklaces. They feature a large crescent-shaped pendant called a *naja*.

CHAPTER 4

THE FAR WESTERN TRIBES

In this photograph taken by Edward S. Curtis, a Hupa female shaman from northwestern California wears shell headbands and necklaces and holds up two small baskets.

In early times, tribes, such as the Chumash, Hupa, Karuk, Pomo, Shasta, and Yurok, tended to be small. Life was hard because much of the land is desert. Acorns and seeds were a major part of the diet. The tribes traded a type of rock called black obsidian that was good for making sharp blades and arrowheads. They also traded pieces of abalone shell and beads made from shells. Because the desert was so difficult to cross, they did not trade with tribes from other areas.

As with other Native American tribes, storytelling was an important part of their lives. For a long, long time the Miwok have told this story:

After Coyote created the world, he gathered all the animals together to help him decide what people should be like. The animals, except for Coyote, argued. Then each one went off alone, gathered some mud, and started to form a being just like himself. Coyote made a person that was cunning like he was, but walked on two legs and had no fur. The sun set and the stars rose and the animals fell asleep. But Coyote kept working. Just before dawn, Coyote was done. Before the other animals woke up, he breathed life into his person and created mankind.

In addition to telling stories, the people created rock paintings, feather headdresses, carved stone pipes, and intricately carved spoons made from elk antlers. Spanish **missionaries** moved to the area in 1769 and turned the Native people into slaves. Many of them died from overwork. Sadly, much of the art and culture of these tribes was lost.

This Karuk deerskin headdress is topped with flicker and goldfinch feathers. It was worn when performing the brush dance.

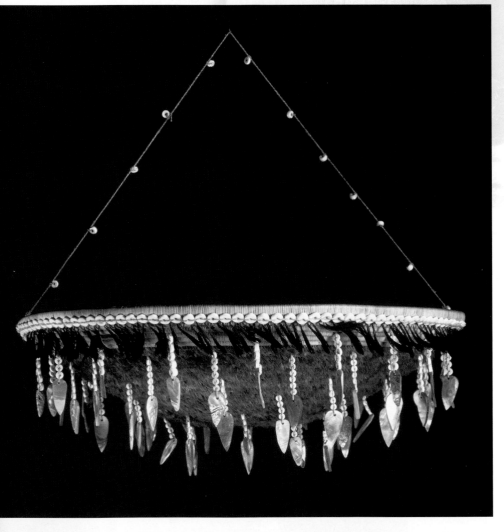

The Pomo made baskets covered with feathers to hang from the ceiling and be admired. Traditionally, they gave these baskets as gifts. This basket, made during the 1800s, is decorated with shell beads and mother-of-pearl pendants.

The Far Western tribes used baskets to collect and store acorns and seeds, cook in, and eat out of. They made basket traps to catch fish. They even carried their babies in baskets. Baskets were also used in ceremonies and as decorations.

In 1908, Elizabeth Conrad Hickox and her daughter Louisa Hickox began selling their baskets through an art dealer named Grace Nicholson. Many museums and collectors bought their work. During the 1930s, Carrie Bethel of the Mono Lake Paiute tribe sold her baskets to tourists in Yosemite National Park.

From 1895 to 1925, Louisa Keyser of the Washoe tribe from Lake Tahoe created baskets for The Cohn Emporium, a store in Carson City, Nevada. The store owner called her Datsolalee, a made-up name that means "big hips." He told people that Keyser was a princess because he thought that title would help him sell her work.

Louisa Keyser is famous for her *degikup* baskets. In this style, the coils of the basket bell out from a small round base then curve back in to the opening in the top. In the photograph, the fourth basket from the left is a *degikup* basket.

In 1883, Sarah Winnemucca published her book *Life Among the Piutes.* In it she describes the customs of her tribe and the hardships caused by white people. By the late 1800s, most of the Paiute land in Nevada had been taken over, and the tribe was forced to move to Washington State.

CHAPTER 5

THE NORTHWESTERN TRIBES

Starting about 3000 B.C.E., the people of the Northwest lived in small fishing camps in the summer. Fish, game, berries, and roots were plentiful, and they gathered enough food to last through the winter. The winter months were spent in longhouses, buildings that were made from cedar logs.

The people of the Northwest tribes see themselves as descendants of different spiritual animals. The Tlingit are either from the Raven **clan** or the Wolf clan. The Haida are from the Raven or Eagle clan, and

Abalone shell was used to make the eyes and teeth in this Tsimshian eagle crest headdress.

the Tsimshian are Bear, Raven, Eagle, or Wolf. These animals show up often in Northwest art.

Originally, totem poles were support posts, then corner posts, for houses. In the late 19th century, freestanding totem poles, some as tall as 50 feet (15.2 m), were built in front of houses. The carvings on the poles showed the status of the people who lived inside by telling the family's spiritual history. The Kwakiutl made another, smaller type of totem pole. These served as memorials to chiefs who had died.

In the 1790s, Europeans arrived in the Northwest. With them, they brought goods to trade—and smallpox, mumps, measles, scarlet fever, and influenza. It was the first time Native Americans had ever been exposed to these diseases. Many of them got sick and died. In the mid-1700s, there were about 200,000 Native Americans living in the Northwest. By the mid-1800s, there were only 40,000.

Chief Sou-i-hat's house and totem pole in Alaska, about 1908

During performances, dancers pull strings attached to their masks to make the mask open up and reveal the figure inside. These are called "transformation" masks.

The traditional stories of the Kwakiutl people are filled with tales of supernatural beings. Kwakiutl artists carve elaborate masks of these beings. The masks are used in dances performed at feasts called potlatches. The word potlatch comes from a Nootka word that means "gift." A family holds a potlatch to celebrate its wealth, a birth, a marriage, the naming of a chief, or the raising of a new totem pole. At a potlatch, guests eat and listen to speeches about the family. Dancers and singers act out family stories. At the end of the potlatch, the guests receive expensive gifts as payment for attending.

During the winter, ceremonial dances, such as Hamat'sa, or the cannibal dance, are performed at Kwakiutl potlatches. In this dance, four masked men portray cannibal birds, and a young man acts as if he is crazed with cannibal power. At the end of the dance, the family elders show their powers over the supernatural and cure the young man of his desire for human flesh.

Willie Seaweed was a woodcarver who is best known for his masks. He was also a Kwakiutl chief. In 1884, the Canadian government outlawed potlatches and their songs and dances. Seaweed worked to help keep the traditions alive until 1951, when the law was finally changed. In the photograph at left, he is holding a *tlakwa*, an engraved sheet of copper shaped like a shield, which he made.

As in other areas, the women of the Northwest tribes made the clothing. Traditionally, blankets, which women wove from strips of cedar bark, were worn around the shoulders. Women even made bark hats that were woven so tightly that they were waterproof.

Chilkat weaving developed in Alaska during the 1800s. Using mountain goat wool and cedar bark, Tlingit women wove beautiful blankets and tunics. The images on the blankets stand for animals. In the old days, men usually carved or painted these designs on wood. Then the women copied them on the blankets. Chilkat blankets became very popular and were traded all along the Northwest coast.

Chilkat tunics and blankets are worn during important occasions such as potlatches.

Button blankets first appeared in the 1800s. These blankets were made from European cloth and imported mother-of-pearl buttons. Usually, button blankets display family **crests**. They are worn for ceremonial occasions, and, in the past, were given away at potlatches.

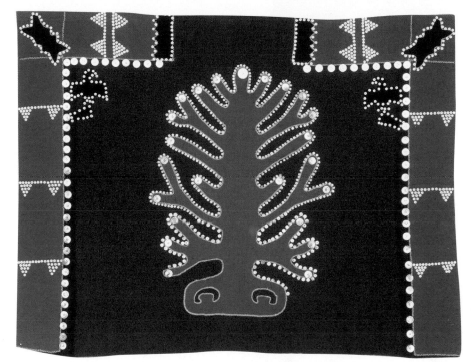

The image on this Kwakiutl button blanket pictures the cedar tree, or Gwa'ka'lee'ka'la, the tree of life.

Christine Quintasket was born in a canoe on the Kootenai River. She started reading novels while still a teenager. When she began writing, she took the name Mourning Dove. In 1927, she became the first Native American woman to publish a novel. The book, called *Co-ge-we-a, the Half Blood*, is about the struggles of a young woman who is half white and half Native American.

CHAPTER 6

THE ARCTIC PEOPLES

By 2000 B.C.E., people had settled in small groups in Alaska and as far north as Greenland. The Inuit, Inupiaq, Yup'ik, and Aleut people of the Arctic region have always lived hard lives. Traditionally, these people lived by hunting fish, walrus, seals, caribou, musk oxen, and birds. In the summer months, they collected as much food as they could to last them through the long, cold months of winter.

Even though the Arctic people had very little to work with, they were very good at creating all the things they needed to survive. As early as C.E. 600, Punuk men carved snow goggles to protect their eyes from the bright light that bounced off the snow. Inuit women made *amautiks*, warm

In this photograph from the late 1920s, Kenowun, a Cup'ig woman from Nunivak Island, Alaska, wears a beaded nose ornament as well as necklaces, earrings, and labrets (ornaments worn through piercings in or below the lips).

Made in the early 1900s, this beaded *amautik* was meant to be worn on special occasions. The caribou fur is on the inside, so the *amautik* would have been worn under another parka with the fur on the outside.

coats with pouches in the back to hold their babies. It required great skill to cut and sew the caribou skin used to make these coats. Beads did not become popular until about 1860, when white whalers began to spend the winter in Hudson Bay.

Together, men and women built boats called kayaks. The men built the frame from driftwood. Then the women sewed walrus or seal skins tightly together and fitted them over the frame. While they worked, they sang and prayed. These kayaks were so well made that men used them to hunt whales! Today, people all over the world go boating in kayaks.

Tools and weapons from the Arctic area are often beautifully carved. In ancient times, people made drills from walrus ivory and covered them with scenes from daily life. No one is sure why the drills are decorated. Spears were carved with figures meant to attract the spirits of the animals that would be hunted with them.

Shamans carved masks from wood, or they designed masks, which were then made by others in the community. People wore the masks during ceremonies. Often, these ceremonies were related to hunting. The people sang, danced, and told stories to please the spirits of the animals. If the animals were pleased, they would allow themselves to be hunted.

This Yup'ik mask, made during the 1800s, represents a spirit being. It may be a Tunghat, one of the spirits that could help hunters if it chose to.

After 1890 and the Alaskan gold rush, carving became an art form to sell to visitors. Angokwazhuk, who became known as Happy Jack, made his living creating carvings in walrus ivory. Angokwazhuk learned to make scrimshaw, an engraving done on ivory, from white sailors on a whaling boat. In his work, Angokwazhuk used both Native American designs and the ones he learned on the ship. He became one of the most well-known carvers in all of Alaska.

A Cup'ig ivory carver from Nunivak Island, Alaska, is working on a walrus tusk in this photograph, which was taken in the late 1920s.

Actor Ray Mala played leading roles in a number of action movies and had featured roles on television. Born in Alaska to an Inupiaq mother and a white father, Mala ran away from boarding school in 1930 to work as a cameraman. Three years later, he starred in a movie called *Eskimo*.

CHAPTER 7

NATIVE AMERICAN
ART TODAY

Many Native American tribes have centers of culture in Oklahoma. Others have centers on or near their ancestral lands, or in cities such as Santa Fe, New York City, and Chicago. Native peoples gather together to celebrate their culture at powwows. They perform dances and songs, speak their native language, and pass on their heritage to future generations.

Teri Greeves, who is of Kiowa and Comanche descent, works in beads, but she takes a more modern approach, as in her beaded high-top sneakers.

Many of today's artists continue to work in the traditions of their ancestors. Lois Gutierrez and Dorothy Torivio are potters. Clarissa Hudson makes button and Chilkat blankets in the Northwest tradition. Sadie Curtis weaves in the Navajo tradition. Beadwork artists, such as Eva McAdams of the Shoshone people, create traditional floral designs on moccasins. Richard Hunt, a Kwakiutl artist, carves masks and totem poles.

In 2004, The Smithsonian Institution's National Museum of the American Indian opened in Washington, D.C. The building and its landscape were designed by a team of Native Americans, including Blackfoot architect Douglas Cardinal and Cherokee and Choctaw architect Johnpaul Jones. The collection includes work from almost 900 different tribes.

The museum's cultural resource center in Suitland, Maryland, allows Native visitors to use objects in the collection for traditional ceremonies. In this way, the museum not only preserves Native American art and culture, but also helps keep traditions alive.

The National Museum of the American Indian in Washington, D.C.

Today's Native American artists have gained recognition for their work in many fields. Painter Jaune Quick-to-See Smith, a member of the Flathead tribe, has shown her work all over the world. Shelley Niro, a Mohawk, is well known for her fine art photography. James Luna, of the Luiseno people, is an installation and performance artist.

Jock Soto, who is of Navajo heritage, has gained an international reputation as a principal dancer with the New York City Ballet. A member of the Muskogee tribe, Joy Harjo is an award-winning poet and the lead singer in her own band. Other popular singers of Native American background include Rita Coolidge, Buffy Sainte Marie, and Cher.

Jock Soto is shown dancing with Wendy Whelan in the New York City Ballet production of *Polyphonia* by Christopher Wheeldon.

Trade (Gifts for Trading Land with White People), 1992, by Jaune Quick-to-See Smith.
In this triptych (three-paneled artwork), Smith uses "cowboys-and-Indians" toys, baseball caps from such teams as the Cleveland Indians, and other objects to call attention to racist images of Native Americans, as well as the purchase of Native American lands for cheap trinkets.

In 1969, writer N. Scott Momaday won the Pulitzer Prize for his novel *House Made of Dawn*. Other popular authors include Louise Erdrich, Sherman Alexie, and Martin Cruz Smith. Erdrich and Alexie write novels about the lives of Native Americans today. Alexie also writes poetry and screenplays. Smith's best-known novels are mysteries featuring Arkady Renko, a Russian detective. In addition to writing books, Joseph Bruchac practices the art of storytelling.

All over the world, Native American art—both old and new—is appreciated for its beauty, sense of history, and lively spirit.

ca. 6000 B.C.E. Native people settle in Southwest

3000 B.C.E. Small artworks placed in burial mounds east of the Mississippi River; native people in Northwest begin to live in fishing camps in summer and longhouses in winter

1500 B.C.E. Tobacco first used in religious rites

300 B.C.E. Anasazi people begin to farm in the Southwest

C.E. 400 Native people of the Southwest begin to make pottery

1580s French traders first visit East Coast of North America

1598 Spanish colonists bring horses, cattle, and sheep to New Mexico

1628-30 Spanish missionaries settle among Pueblo people

1650 Kiowa people acquire horses

1769 Spanish missionaries move to California and enslave local Native Americans

1770 Sequoyah born (d. 1843)

1790s Europeans arrive in the Northwest bringing diseases that kill thousands of Native Americans

1821 Sequoyah's writing system approved by Cherokee tribal council

1828 *The Cherokee Phoenix*, the first Native American newspaper, is published

ca. 1829-1850 Louisa Keyser (Datsolalee) born (d. 1925)

1830 Indian Removal Act passed; Atsidi Sani born (d. 1870)

1838 Trail of Tears, forced march of Cherokee from Georgia to Oklahoma

ca. 1842 Sarah Winnemucca born (d. 1891)

1860 Nampeyo born (d. 1942)

1864 Navajo people forced to move to Bosque Redondo reservation (return to homeland in 1868)

ca. 1870 Angokwazhuk (Happy Jack) born (d. 1918)

1873 Elizabeth Conrad Hickox born (d. 1947); Willie Seaweed born (d. 1967)

1880 Buffalo nearly become extinct because of overhunting

1883 Sarah Winnemucca publishes *Life Among the Piutes*

1884 Canadian government outlaws potlatches (repealed 1951); John Stands-In-Timber born (d. 1967)

1887 Maria (Montoya) Martinez born (d. 1980); Julian Martinez born (d. 1943)

1888 Christine Quintasket (Mourning Dove) born (d. 1936)

1896 Louisa Hickox born (d. 1962)

1898 Carrie Bethel born (d. 1974)

1906 Roy Mala born (d. 1952)

1924 Indian Citizenship Act grants voting rights to Native Americans in some states

1928 Eva McAdams born

1930 Sadie Curtis born

1934 Douglas Cardinal born; N. Scott Momaday born

1940 Jaune Quick-to-See Smith born

1941 Johnpaul Jones born; Buffy Sainte Marie born

1942 Joseph Bruchac born; Martin Cruz Smith born

1944 Rita Coolidge born

1946 Cher born; Dorothy Torivio born

1950 James Luna born

mid-1900s Cheyenne creation story first written down by John Stands In Timber

1951 Joy Harjo born; Richard Hunt born

1954 Louise Erdrich born; Shelley Niro born

1957 Utah is the last state to grant voting rights to Native Americans

1965 Jock Soto born

1966 Sherman Alexie born

1969 N. Scott Momaday is first Native American author to win Pulitzer Prize

2004 The National Museum of the American Indian opens in Washington, D.C.

archaeologist a person who finds and studies objects from peoples and cultures of the past

chant to speak words or sing a song over and over again, rhythmically but in the same tone of voice; the words or song chanted

clan a family group descended from the same ancestor

crest a stylized picture or pictures adopted as a symbol by a group of people

kachina the spirit of a living thing

kachina tihu a carving representing a kachina

kayak a canoe-like boat that has one or two small openings for a person or persons to sit in and is propelled by a double-sided paddle

missionary a priest, minister, or other church official who travels to new places in order to teach the people who live there his or her religion

potlatch a feast held by Native Americans of the Northwest Coast at which the chief or other person who holds the potlatch gives gifts to the guests

reservation land set aside by the government for Native Americans

shaman a priest or holy person

shard a broken piece of pottery

tribe a social group of people, which can include families and clans of different generations, together with dependents or adopted strangers

Byrd Baylor, *When Clay Sings*, Aladdin, 1987

Joseph Bruchac, *Between Earth & Sky: Legends of Native American Sacred Places*, Voyager Books, 1999

Michael Chanin, *The Chief's Blanket*, H. J. Kramer, 1998

Gerald Dawavendewa, *The Butterfly Dance* (Tales of the People), Abbeville Press, 2001

Joy Harjo, *The Good Luck Cat*, Harcourt Children's Books, 2000

Arlene Hirschfelder, *Artists and Craftspeople* (American Indian Lives), Facts on File, 1994

Lisa Larrabee, *Grandmother Five Baskets*, Harbinger House, 2000

Cynthia Leitich Smith, *Jingle Dancer*, HarperCollins, 2000

Reavis Moore, *Native Artists of North America: Profiles of Five American Indian Artists, Highlighting Their Talents and Exploring Their Roles Within Their Tribes*, John Muir Publications, 1995

Web Sites

Native Languages of the Americas
Facts for Kids
http://www.native-languages.org/kids.htm

Native American Website for Children
New Haven Unified School District, California
http://www.nhusd.k12.ca.us/ALVE/NativeAmerhome.html/nativeamhome.html

First Americans
Karen Martin, Muskogee Nation
http://jamaica.u.arizona.edu/ic/kmartin/School/index.htm

ACKNOWLEDGMENTS

The editors wish to thank the following organizations and individuals for permission to reprint the literary quotes and to reproduce the images in this book. Every effort has been made to obtain permission from the owners of all materials. Any errors that may have been made are unintentional and will be corrected in future printings if notice is given to the publisher.

Cover: Mask with humanoid face, side view/Bella Coola Culture, Northwest Coast of America/Alder wood and red cedar bark/Provincial Museum, Victoria, British Columbia, Canada/Werner Forman/Art Resource, NY

Title page, p. 33 (background): Masked Kwakiutl dancers at winter ceremony, ca. 1914/Edward S. Curtis (1868–1952), photographer/Library of Congress

p. 4: Ceremonial mask/Bella Coola Culture, Northwest Coast of America (19th century)/ Wood/Museum of Mankind, London, Great Britain/Erich Lessing/ Art Resource, NY

p. 5 (left): Eskimo in kayak, ca. 1900–1930/Lomen Bros., photographers/Library of Congress; **(right):** Tipi/Ablestock

p. 6: Human-effigy Pipe (SC 10)/Adena Culture, Early Woodland period, 500 B.C.E.–C.E. 1/Ohio Historical Society

p. 7 (top): Copper Falcon/Mound City Group/Courtesy of the National Park Service; **(bottom):** Serpent Mound (SC 804)/Adams County, Ohio/Ohio Historical Society

p. 8: Beaver bowl, 18th century/wood/Kaskaskia?/ Peabody Museum, Harvard University, Photo 99-12-10/52998 T1231

p. 9 (right): Se-Quo-Yah, ca. 1836/Hand-colored lithograph from a painting by Charles Bird King/History of the Tribes of North America by Thomas L. McKenney and James Hall, 1838–1844/Library of Congress; **(left):** Robert Lindneux/The Trail of Tears/Woolarock Museum, Bartlesville, Oklahoma

p. 10: Bag, ca. 1890/Wool yarn, nettle fiber, buckskin tie/11 x 14 3/4 x 2 in. (27.9 x 37.5 x 5.1 cm)/Mesquakie/Founders Society Purchase/Photograph © 1992 The Detroit Institute of Arts

p. 11: Moccasins, ca. 1875/Deerskin, buffalo hide, glass beads/Length: 10 1/2 in. (26.67 cm)/Nebraska/Founders Society Purchase/Photograph © 1992 The Detroit Institute of Arts

p. 12: Native Americans in a Snowstorm/Hand-colored woodcut/Copyright © North Wind/North Wind Picture Archives/All rights reserved

p. 13: Seated Male Figure/Wood/13 1/4 in. (33.66 cm)/Caddoan Culture (Spiro), C.E. 1200–1350/Catalogue No. 448892, Department of Anthropology, Smithsonian Institution

p. 14: Shirt, 1870s/Deer hide, pigment, wool, glass beads (seed), horse hair, human hair, porcupine quills/Sioux/South Dakota/Buffalo Bill Historical Center, Cody, Wyoming; Adolf Spohr Collection, Gift of Larry Sheerin/NA.202.598

p. 15 (right): Tsistsistas (Cheyenne) feather headdress, ca. 1870/Fort Sill, Oklahoma?/Length: 198.5 cm/Photo by David Heald/Courtesy, National Museum of the American Indian, Smithsonian Institution (20/5318); **(bottom):** Chief Joseph, Nez Percé, ca. 1903/Edward S. Curtis (1868–1952), photographer/Library of Congress

p. 16: Buffalo robe, ca. 1835/Upper Missouri River area/Catalogue No. 2130, Department of Anthropology, Smithsonian Institution

p. 17 (top): Arapoosh (Sore Belly, Absaroke [Crow])/Buffalo hide shield, before 1830/Montana/Diam. 61.5 cm/Photo by David Heald/Courtesy, National Museum of the American Indian, Smithsonian Institution (11/7680); **(bottom):** Etahdleuh Doanmoe/Two Warriors Wearing Face Paint and Costumes, Including Blankets, Carrying Feather Fans and Riding Horses with Trappings, March 1880/Painting/Inventory No. 8517800, Department of Anthropology, Smithsonian Institution

p. 18: Antelope House, Cañon del Muerto/Edward S. Curtis (1868–1952), photographer/Library of Congress

p. 19 (top): Effigy figure, ca. 10th–13th century/Pottery/Height: 15 3/4 in./Anasazi/ Inv.: 70.10/The Newark Museum/Art Resource, NY; **(bottom):** A Navajo shaman preparing colored sands for use in treatment of a sick child, ca. 1951/Library of Congress

p. 20: Roosevelt black-on-white bird effigy canteen with Pinedale style, 1300–1350/Salado, Tonto-Roosevelt Province, Medler Ruin/Gift of Gila Pueblo Foundation/Collected by Hughes and Dennis, Catalog No. GP8240/Arizona State Museum/University of Arizona/Janelle Weakly, photographer

p. 21 (top): Nampeyo decorating pottery, ca. 1903/Library of Congress; **(bottom):** Photograph of Julian and Maria Martinez/Courtesy Museum of New Mexico/Negative No. 40814

p. 22: Germantown eye dazzler blanket/rug, ca. 1885–1895/Wool and cotton/151 cm. x 92 cm. x 0.2 cm/Navajo/Peabody Museum, Harvard University, Photo 995-29-10/73899 T2164.1

p. 23: Navajo blanket and belt weavers, ca. 1982–93/James Mooney (1861–1921), photographer

p. 24: Kachina Doll (Chilchi). Collected in 1903. Pueblo, Zuni/Wood, pigment, wool, hide, cotton, tin, 22 1/2 x 9 x 8 in. (57.2 x 22.9 x 20.3 cm)/Brooklyn Museum. 03.325.4631. Museum Expedition 1903, Museum Collection Fund

p. 25 (left): Navajo silversmith with examples of his work and tools, ca. 1880/Ben Wittick, photographer/American Indian Select List number 37/U.S. National Archives & Records Administration; **(right):** Navajo squash blossom necklace, 1910–25 (silver), American School (20th century)/© Museum of Fine Arts, Houston, Texas, USA, Gift of Mrs. O. S. Simpson, Jr./Bridgeman Art Library

p. 26: Hupa female shaman, ca. 1923/Edward S. Curtis (1868–1952), photographer/Library of Congress

p. 27: Karok Dance Hat, 19th century/feathers, deerskin/Height: 19.05 cm/ Northern California/Peabody Museum, Harvard University, Photo 08-4-10/73364 T1220.1

p. 28: Pomo Basket/Courtesy of the Autry National Center, Southwest Museum, Los Angeles. 811.G.1683 (CT.294)

p. 29 (top): Louisa Keyser (Datsolalee), ca. 1899/Library of Congress; **(bottom):** Sarah Winnemucca/Nevada Historical Society

p. 30: Eagle crest headdress with eye inlaid with abalone shell/Tsimshian Culture/Inv. 160-1/Provincial Museum, Victoria, British Columbia, Canada/Werner Forman/Art Resource, NY

p. 31 (top left): Chief Sou-i-hat's house and totem pole, ca. 1908/Alaska/Library of Congress; **(right):** Totem pole/Ablestock

p. 32: Kwakiutl, revelation mask/American Museum of Natural History, New York, USA/Copyright unknown/ Bridgeman Art Library

p. 33: Willie Seaweed (Heyhlamas, or The One Able To Set Things Right, or Siwiti), a Kwakwakawakw (Kwakiutl) chief, 1951/Blunden Harbor, British Columbia, Canada/Photo by William R. Heick/Courtesy, National Museum of the American Indian, Smithsonian Institution (P19648)

p. 34: Chilkat Tlingit tunic with bear design, 19th century/Alaska/Photo by David Heald/Courtesy, National Museum of the American Indian, Smithsonian Institution (00/7076)

p. 35 (top): Kwakwakawakw (Kwakiutl) decorated blue trade button blanket, late 19th/early 20th century/Cape Mudge, Vancouver Island, British Columbia, Canada/182 x 139.7 cm/Photo by David Heald/Courtesy, National Museum of the American Indian, Smithsonian Institution (11/5129); **(bottom):** Christine Quintasket (Mourning Dove)/The Newberry Library, Chicago, Illinois

p. 36: Kenowun, a Nunivak woman/ Edward S. Curtis (1868–1952), photographer/Library of Congress

p. 37 (right): Aivilingmiut Igulik amautik (woman's parka), early 20th century/Lake Yathkeid, Hudson Bay, Canada/Length: 123.5 cm/Photo by David Heald/Courtesy, National Museum of the American Indian, Smithsonian Institution (13/7198); **(left):** Eskimo man in kayak preparing to throw spear// Edward S. Curtis (1868–1952), photographer/Library of Congress

p. 38: Native American, Mask (NEGAKFOK), early 20th Century. Alaska, Yup'ik peoples, Kuskokwirn River. Wood, paint, feathers; Height 45 1/4 in./The Metropolitan Museum of Art, The Michael C. Rockefeller Memorial Collection, Purchase, Nelson A. Rockefeller Gift, 1961 (1978.412.76) Photograph © 1984 The Metropolitan Museum of Art

p. 39 (right): Nunivak ivory carver// Edward S. Curtis (1868–1952), photographer/Library of Congress; **(left):** Roy Mala/Photo by Metro-Goldwin-Mayer/Alaska State Library/Skinner Foundation. Photographs, Alaska Steamship Company, 1890s–1940s/ASL-PCA-44/Identifier ASL-P44-03-131

p. 40: Teri Greeves (Kiowa), beaded hightop sneakers entitled "Kiowa Ah-Day," 2004. Lander, Wyoming/Photo by Walter Larrimore/Courtesy, National Museum of the American Indian, Smithsonian Institution (26/3325)

p. 41: East façade of the National Museum of the American Indian, 21 September 2004. Washington, DC/Photo by R. A. Whiteside/Courtesy, National Museum of the American Indian, Smithsonian Institution

p. 42: Jock Soto and Wendy Whelan of New York City Ballet performing Christopher Wheeldon's Polyophonia/New York City Ballet/Photograph © Paul Kolnik

p. 43: Jaune Quick-to-See Smith (American, b. 1940), Trade (Gifts for Trading Land with White People), 1992/Oil and mixed media/60 x 170 inches/Chrysler Museum of Art, Norfolk, VA, Museum Purchase (93.2)/Art copyright © Jaune Quick-to-See Smith

Background, pp. 4, 13, 25, 30: Ablestock
Background, pp. 6, 12, 15, 19, 24, 26, 28: Library of Congress